The Fun of Cooking

The
Fun of
Cooking

Jill Krementz

Alfred A. Knopf, New York, 1985

Library of Congress Cataloging in Publication Data

Krementz, Jill.
The fun of cooking.

Summary: A collection of recipes, illustrated with photographs, for a
variety of dishes including pumpkin pie, cucumber sushi, homemade
pasta, granola, and lemon chicken.
1. Cookery—Juvenile literature. [1. Cookery]
I. Title.
TX652.5.K74   1985   641.5'123   85-40332
ISBN 0-394-54808-6

Manufactured in the United States of America
FIRST EDITION

For Lily
with a kiss
and a hug
and a squeeze

Helpful Hints for Cooking Safely

Tie your hair back if it is long. Roll up floppy sleeves.

Turn handles of saucepans on the range to the side to avoid knocking over pans.

Wipe up spills on floor right away so you don't slip and fall.

Be very careful with anything electric. Turn off a mixer—better still, unplug it—before you put in the beaters or take them out. When you disconnect an electric appliance, don't pull the cord. Pull the plug.

Be very careful handling knives. Don't ever pick up a knife by the blade. Always move the blade away from you when cutting or peeling. Use a firm surface when cutting—don't use a plate which can slip away from you. And most important of all, keep your eye on what you're doing at all times.

Be careful with your fingertips when grating cheeses.

When lighting the oven of a gas range, keep your face as far away as possible. Younger children should let a grown-up do this.

Always use thick, dry potholders when touching a pot that may be hot.

Be especially careful draining foods cooked in large amounts of hot water (like spaghetti). The steam can cause a bad burn.

Watch out when you add food to hot oil or butter—it can spatter and burn you.

If you fill your sink with sudsy water to clean utensils, don't add knives or food processor blades. When you reach in, you may cut yourself on the blade. A child should not use a food processor without careful supervision.

Make sure you turn off the heat on your oven or range when you're finished cooking.

Contents

Lee's Chocolate Mousse

ONE 8-INCH ROUND CAKE

INGREDIENTS

8 ounces (8 squares) sweetened chocolate
1 ounce (1 square) unsweetened chocolate
4 eggs, separated
4 tablespoons sugar
4 tablespoons milk
2 cups heavy cream
1 teaspoon vanilla extract
3-ounce package containing 24 ladyfingers
    (unfilled)
Fresh strawberries or raspberries—for
    decoration (optional)

UTENSILS

3 mixing bowls
double boiler
electric beater
measuring spoons
rubber spatula
8-inch springform mold

INSTRUCTIONS

1. Place largest of three empty bowls in freezer so it will be cold when you're ready to whip cream.
2. Melt chocolate in top of double boiler.
3. Beat egg yolks in second bowl while adding sugar.
4. Add milk to chocolate, mix together, and then pour into bowl containing sugar and yolk mixture.
5. Clean beaters and in third bowl beat egg whites until stiff and shiny. Remember—egg whites and heavy cream expand when beaten, so make sure your bowls are not too small.
6. Make sure beaters are again clean and dry. Pour heavy cream into chilled bowl, add vanilla, and whip until stiff.
7. Fold egg whites into chocolate mixture. Then fold this into the whipped cream.
8. Prepare springform mold with ladyfingers around edge. They will stand up by themselves. An 8-inch mold will take twenty-two ladyfingers. Don't use a larger mold.
9. Pour mixture into mold and chill in refrigerator for 3 hours. Take out of refrigerator when ready to serve, remove sides of springform mold, and decorate, if you wish, with strawberries or raspberries.

Lee, age fifteen

I love to cook. When I was about six or seven, I'd come home from school and sit around the kitchen and help Mom with little things like chopping vegetables and boiling potatoes. I usually got home earlier than my older sister and brother, so I'd always do my homework in the kitchen while my mother cooked dinner. I think cooking's a lot of fun, and it gives me a real sense of accomplishment when I make something that really tastes good and everybody likes.

I always break up the chocolate into little pieces before I put it into the top of a double boiler because that way it melts more easily.

While the chocolate is melting, I separate the eggs. The easiest way to do this is to dump the whole egg into the palm of your hand and let the white part dribble through your fingers.

I beat the yolks with an electric beater or a whisk, and when they're mixed, I add the sugar and beat until light and creamy.

When the chocolate is melted, add the milk to the pot, mix it in, and then add it to the bowl holding the egg yolks. Stir with a rubber spatula until the mixture is smooth. Put the bowl aside for the time being and, using another bowl, beat the egg whites until they're stiff. Be *sure* the mixer blades and the bowl are clean and totally dry or the whites will never whip. There's a good test you can do. Turn the beater upside down and if the whites don't flop over, they're stiff enough.

Now it's time to get the chilled bowl out of the freezer. You chill the bowl so the cream won't curdle and turn to butter. Another way for cream to turn to butter is to overbeat, so beat it only until it is thick and you can make soft peaks with the cream as you lift the beaters.

Next, using a rubber spatula, fold the egg whites into the chocolate. Do this very gently —and quickly—using as few strokes as possible so the egg whites will stay fluffy and full of air. Be sure not to mix the whites in—just fold them. Now, using this same technique, fold the combined egg-white and chocolate mixture into the whipped cream.

I usually enlist my brother Jay, or whoever's around, to help me with the last step, which is to pour the final mixture into the mold. It takes about three hours to chill in the refrigerator. If I need it fast, I put it into the freezer instead for about thirty minutes and then into the refrigerator for an hour and a half. I like to decorate my mousse with strawberries or raspberries before serving.

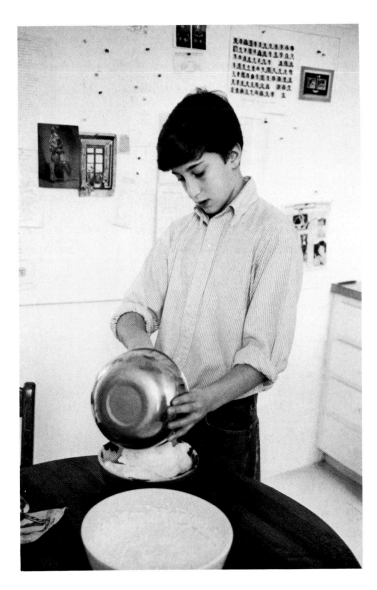

Jill's Matzo Ball Soup

SERVES 8

Chicken Soup

INGREDIENTS
1 soup chicken (4–6 pounds), cut into quarters
2 onions, peeled and sliced
3 carrots, peeled and sliced
1 tomato, cored
3 sprigs parsley
3 stalks celery, including leaves
1 sprig fresh dill, or ½ teaspoon dill weed
Salt and pepper to taste
Water to cover chicken

UTENSILS
sharp knife
4-quart pot with lid
cutting board
wooden spoon

vegetable scraper
measuring spoons
large strainer

INSTRUCTIONS
1. Clean chicken thoroughly.
2. Place in deep pot with other ingredients. Bring water to a boil, reduce heat, and simmer for 2½–3 hours, or until chicken is tender.
3. Remove chicken and strain soup.
4. Serve hot with matzo balls and with pieces of chicken or carrots, if desired.

Matzo Balls

INGREDIENTS
2 tablespoons chicken fat, melted (can be bought at any kosher butcher)
2 eggs, slightly beaten
½ cup (preferably less) matzo meal
1 teaspoon salt
2 tablespoons ice water

UTENSILS
fork
mixing bowl with cover (or you can use aluminum foil)
measuring cup

measuring spoons
1 small bowl (for water to dip your hands into)
2–3-quart pot

INSTRUCTIONS
1. Gently combine fat and eggs in mixing bowl with fork. Don't overbeat or matzo balls will lose fluffy quality.
2. Add matzo meal and salt. (The key is to use as little matzo meal as possible—the least means the lightest matzo ball.) When well blended, add ice water.
3. Cover bowl and refrigerate for at least 2 hours or overnight—the longer the mixture is to be refrigerated, the less matzo meal is needed.
4. Dip your hands in water to moisten and form little matzo balls.
5. The matzo balls can be cooked in either a 2–3-quart pot of boiling water or in the clear, strained chicken soup. Bring liquid to boil; reduce heat. Place matzo balls gently in simmering liquid. Cover pot and cook for 20–25 minutes.

Jill, age eleven

I started cooking when I was five. I'd help my mom, or my grandma when I was visiting her. And I did a lot of baking with my dad. It's fun following recipes and seeing how things work out. And it's fun to eat whatever you make. My grandmother is a wonderful cook, and she taught my father how to cook when he was my age. We have a family recipe for matzo ball soup and we usually make it for Passover and Rosh Hashana, but it's so good we make it other times too.

You have to prepare the soup first because it has to simmer for about three hours. I begin by washing my hands so they're clean before I touch any food. Then I rinse a whole chicken that has been cut up into pieces. Peeling onions is a lot easier if you cut off both ends first. The carrots have to have both their ends cut off too. Since I like to have a few sliced carrots in my soup, I peel them with a vegetable scraper and slice them into small pieces. With the tomato you just remove the core, and the only thing you have to do with the parsley and the celery is to take off the rubber bands and trim the bottoms.

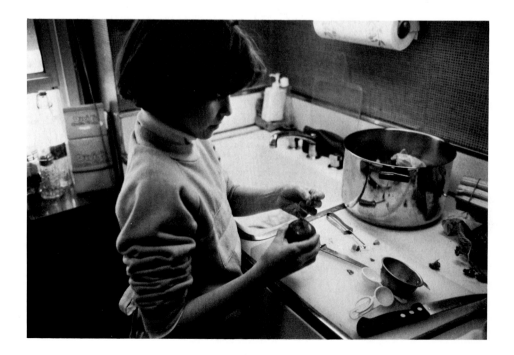

Since it's very important to wash everything that goes into the pot, I make my soup standing right next to the sink. I like to add a little seasoning, and I use coarse salt, but you can use the regular kind. I also add some pepper from a pepper mill—about six grinds. When everything's ready, I fill the pot with enough water to cover the ingredients and put it on the stove over medium heat.

After I clean up, I make the mixture for the matzo balls using the recipe on the matzo meal box. While I'm beating the eggs in the bowl, my grandma slowly adds the matzo meal. You have to be especially careful to scrape the edges of the bowl so there won't be any lumps. When the matzo ball mixture is ready, it has to be refrigerated, and even though the recipe calls for only twenty minutes, Grandma says, "I say more—about two hours." I go along with Grandma on this because she's such a wonderful cook.

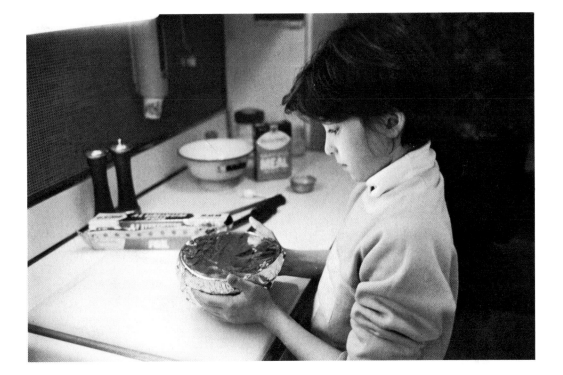

It's good to cover the matzo ball mixture with aluminum foil so the other odors in the refrigerator don't settle on our matzo balls.

Then, while the soup is still simmering and the matzo meal mixture is chilling, Grandma and I play cards or talk. I think that my grandmother and I have a very special relationship because of all the fun we have cooking. If you're really close to a person, you can get even closer just by preparing a meal together.

Making the matzo balls is the most fun of all. It helps to have a little bowl of cold water handy to keep my hands moist. I scoop up a piece of matzo ball mixture and roll it into a perfect ball between my wet hands. The perfect matzo ball is a little bigger than a marble but smaller than a golf ball.

Carefully drop the matzo balls into boiling water and let them cook for about twenty minutes. This is another example where the recipe on the box suggests a different amount of time, but Grandma says twenty minutes is fine. As the matzo balls cook, they get bigger.

At last comes the best part…eating our matzo ball soup. I can't ever get my father to join us—he says he HATES chicken soup because he had too much of it while he was growing up. Fine with me because there's more for us.

Alix's Apple Cinnamon Muffins

10-12 MUFFINS

INGREDIENTS

1 package Betty Crocker's apple cinnamon
    muffin mix
About ½ cup milk
1 egg

UTENSILS

muffin pan
paper baking cups (optional)
can opener for tin inside muffin mix box
measuring cup
mixing bowl
fork
large spoon
potholders

INSTRUCTIONS

1. Preheat oven to 400°F. Grease bottoms of medium muffin cups or use paper baking cups.
2. Open tin containing apple chunks and drain off liquid into measuring cup. Add milk to same measuring cup so that milk and apple liquid combined measure ½ cup.
3. Pour apple-liquid mixture into a mixing bowl, add egg, and mix with fork.
4. Stir in muffin mix just until moistened—batter will be lumpy.
5. With a large spoon fold apple chunks into batter. Fill muffin cups one-half full.
6. Bake until golden brown, about 12 minutes, but every oven varies, so you should check for yourself. Insert a toothpick into a muffin; if it comes out clean, muffins are cooked. Using potholders, remove from oven.

Alix, age six

What I love most about cooking is baking. I like using mixes because it's quicker and I get to eat the results sooner. Sometimes we cook applesauce or popcorn at school, but mostly I cook with Mommy, especially during the summer when we're on vacation. We always try to have a party when there's bad weather, which is a good idea because instead of being scared of thunderstorms I almost look forward to them. My daddy says my apple cinnamon muffins make him feel happy all day, rain or shine.

Whenever you bake something, you have to preheat the oven so the temperature will be right when you start cooking whatever it is you're making. I always peek in first to make sure it's clean and there's nothing inside—like another pan. Mommy lights the oven because I'm not allowed to yet.

If you're working with a mix, you'll find that most of the ingredients are right inside the package except things like eggs and milk. Mommy says it's always best if you measure at eye level. She also says that when you're stirring you shouldn't be too rough on your batter—it's better if it stays a little lumpy.

I love emptying the little tin of apple chunks into my mixing bowl.

It's more fun if you line your muffin pan with baking cups that are all different colors. When I fill them I'm very careful not to get any of the batter on the outside because it will only burn.

My little sister, Bettina, helps me lick the bowl.

I like to serve lemonade with my muffins, and for that I use another mix. I guess you could say we're a "mix family."

Finally I yell, "The muffins are coming," and everyone comes running into the kitchen for a nice homemade party.

Taso's Fresh Garden Salad and Dressing

SERVES 2–6

INGREDIENTS
Swiss chard
1 avocado
2 tomatoes
Parsley
Iceberg lettuce

UTENSILS
sharp knife
salad bowl
measuring cup
jar with top

INSTRUCTIONS
1. Wash and trim vegetables, remove center stems from Swiss chard, cut everything into medium-size pieces, and place in salad bowl.
2. To make dressing, place in jar: lemon juice, olive oil, chopped parsley, vinegar, and oregano. Shake and distribute evenly on salad.
3. Toss salad and serve.

Salad Dressing

Juice of 2 lemons
½ cup olive oil (Pompeian is the closest to Greek olive oil)
Few pinches of chopped parsley
1 shake of vinegar (about ½ teaspoon)
5 shakes of oregano

Taso, age ten

When I was a little baby, my mother would hold me in her arms while she made Greek pastries, and if she made baklava she'd let me stick in the cloves. When I got older, I'd sit on the counter and watch her by the hour. Soon I began to do a little cooking on my own. For example, I'd make up recipes for meals that I'd feed to my puppets and I made chocolate-covered rocks for my little brother, Petros. I'd tell him they were M&Ms and he'd believe me.

Now that I'm older I really do enjoy cooking. Since we have a beautiful garden, it's fun and very convenient to make delicious salads. I begin by cutting a bunch of Swiss chard, and I use the young leaves because they taste sweeter.

I pick the lemons that are the fattest because they have the most juice. The avocados are a little harder to reach, and we use a long pole with a basket on the end. If Papa and Petros are around, all three of us do this together. I'm the catcher.

It's important when making a salad to wash everything *very* carefully. Be sure to cut the white stem out of the Swiss chard, because it's bitter. This is the part that takes the longest and I'd have to say it's pretty boring. All the other stuff whizzes by.

The vegetables have such a beautiful taste when they come out of the garden that it's best to have a light dressing that won't be overpowering. I make mine in a jar because it's easier to shake up. The best trick of all is to toss your salad gently so it doesn't end up on the floor.

Paige's Perfect Dinner
SERVES 4

Fresh Fruit Salad in Melon Basket

INGREDIENTS
2 bananas
2 green apples
2 red apples
1 small bunch green seedless grapes
1 large, ripe (it should smell like a melon) honeydew or
    cantaloupe
1–2 cups orange juice

UTENSILS

paring knife   soup spoon
bowl   mixing spoon
felt-tip pen

INSTRUCTIONS
Peel and slice bananas. Wash and core apples, then cut
into cubes. Wash grapes and put in a bowl along with
apples and bananas. Mark melon with felt-tip pen to make
a basket shape; cut along the line. Scoop out melon seeds
with soup spoon, cut out and cube melon pieces, and add
to other fruit in bowl. Add orange juice, mix well, and
spoon into melon basket. Serve extra fruit alongside.

Burnt Butter Spinach

INGREDIENTS
½ cup water
10-ounce package frozen leaf spinach
1 stick (8 tablespoons) sweet butter
Freshly grated nutmeg
Salt and freshly ground pepper to taste

UTENSILS

measuring cup   linen tea towel
1½-quart saucepan   skillet
colander/strainer   wooden spoon

INSTRUCTIONS
In saucepan bring water to a boil; add spinach and cook
until just thawed, about 10 minutes. Drain spinach in colander, wring out in towel, and set aside. When ready to
serve, melt butter in skillet and brown over medium heat
until it is the color of a brown paper bag. Add spinach, stir
well, and sauté over low heat for about 5 minutes, or until
butter is completely absorbed. Season to taste with nutmeg, salt, and pepper.

Baked Stuffed Potatoes

INGREDIENTS
4 large baking potatoes
3–4 tablespoons butter
About 1 cup milk
2 slices American cheese
Salt, pepper, and paprika to taste

UTENSILS
brush   spoon
fork   mixing bowl
baking sheet lined with   Foley food fork or
    aluminum foil   potato masher
potholders   measuring cup
small paring knife   saucepan

INSTRUCTIONS
Preheat oven to 375°F. Scrub potatoes with brush and
prick skin with fork. Place on lined baking sheet and bake
for about 45 minutes, or until potatoes are soft inside when
tested with a fork. Using potholders, remove potatoes from
oven, cut off tops with knife, scoop out insides with spoon,
and place in bowl. Mash with Foley food fork until there
are no more lumps. Meanwhile, melt butter with milk and
cheese in saucepan over medium heat. Pour milk mixture
into mashed potatoes and stir well. Add salt and pepper to
taste, stuff filling into skins (you can also put a little bit of
potato stuffing on each of four tops), garnish with paprika,
and return to oven for 10–15 minutes, or until hot.

Broiled Fillet of Flounder

INGREDIENTS
4 fillets of flounder, about 6–8 ounces each
Juice of ½ lemon
Freshly ground pepper to taste
1 tablespoon butter
Lemon slices

UTENSILS

paring knife   cutting board
broiler pan   potholders
spatula

INSTRUCTIONS
Preheat broiler. Butter broiler pan so fish doesn't stick.
With paring knife cut "spiny" column out of middle of
each fillet (you can feel it with your finger). Place fillets on
broiler pan, drizzle lemon juice over top, season with pepper, and dot top with butter. Broil for 5–8 minutes, or until
fish is white and flaky. Remove from broiler with potholders and serve. Garnish plate with lemon slices.

Paige, age thirteen

To tell you the truth, I'd much rather cook than eat. My mother has her own cooking school and catering business, so I've been assisting her for as long as I can remember. I started out by washing dishes when I was about three, and by the time I was seven I was helping her with the hors d'oeuvres—I'd stuff the cherry tomatoes and make ribbon sandwiches.

I prefer simple foods, so a perfect meal, as far as I'm concerned, is flounder, burnt butter spinach, baked stuffed potatoes, and a fruit salad for dessert. It tastes good and it doesn't take long to make.

When you're cooking an entire meal, timing is everything, so I always begin by figuring out the proper sequence. In this case, because the potatoes are going to have to cook for about an hour, I start by putting them into the oven.

Then I make the fruit salad, and for this you can use whatever fruits you like best. After it's all cut up and in a bowl, add the orange juice and stir *gently*. If you're too rough, the fruit will end up all over the table and, worse still, the bananas will get all squished.

The hard part is making the melon basket. A felt-tip pen works well to mark the basket shape on the melon. After you've finished carving out the pieces, use a damp cloth to wipe off any ink that still shows. Then spoon out the seeds as well as quite a bit of the melon so there will be plenty of room. You can cut up some of the extra melon and add it to the fruit salad.

I generally use a package of frozen leaf spinach because I think it's as good as the fresh stuff. I cook the spinach following the directions on the box, and after draining it in a colander, I put it in a dish towel and wrap it up in a little ball to squeeze out all the water. If you rinse it under the cold tap for a while it helps, because that way you don't burn your hands. It's important to squeeze out all the excess water for two reasons: one is that watery spinach tastes awful and two is that if you put watery spinach into the hot butter, it'll splatter and you'll burn yourself.

Next comes the burnt butter part, and that's easy. Take one stick of sweet butter and brown it for five to eight minutes over medium heat—not high, because if the butter burns too fast it will stick to the pan and then you won't have enough for the spinach. The reason you use sweet butter is because salted butter will separate. When the butter's nice and brown, add the spinach and sauté over low heat for about five minutes, or until the butter is completely absorbed. I like to grate in a little fresh nutmeg and add salt and pepper as a finishing touch. It can sit on the stove until you're ready to serve.

The biggest worry with potatoes is not overcooking but undercooking. You test them by poking them with a fork; they should feel soft in the middle.

Cut a small lid lengthwise off each potato and save it. Then, using a spoon, scoop the insides out of the jackets and put into bowl for mashing. Be very careful not to rip the potato skins. I usually cradle them in the palm of my hand with a potholder under the potato.

I love to use a Foley food fork, which was given to my mom for her thirteenth birthday by her Aunt Rubye. She got that and a cookbook.

After you've mixed in the butter, milk, and cheese, restuff the potatoes and sprinkle the tops with paprika. Good cooks always sprinkle spices into the palm of one hand and then work from there because that's the only way to control the amount of seasoning.

Fish doesn't take very long so always do it last.

Fillet of fish means it's without bones and skin. Fish have a spiny column—or backbone—and if the store hasn't removed it, you have to. You can feel it with your finger.

After the fillets are washed, I add a few tiny squares of butter and some juice from a lemon wedge.

Now it's time to take out the potatoes and change the oven from bake to broil. Set the timer for five minutes, and while the fish is broiling, reheat your spinach over medium heat. When the five minutes are up, dinner's ready. Enjoy!

Liz's Chocolate Waffles

SERVES 2–4

INGREDIENTS

⅔ cup flour
½ teaspoon baking powder
¼ teaspoon salt
1½ tablespoons unsweetened cocoa
⅓ cup sugar
¼ cup sour cream
3 tablespoons butter, melted
2 eggs, separated
Pinch of cream of tartar

UTENSILS

flour sifter
3 mixing bowls
measuring cups
measuring spoons
small saucepan for melting butter
wooden spoon
electric beater
electric waffle iron
medium-size spoon for transferring
    batter to waffle iron
fork for transferring waffles to
    serving dish

INSTRUCTIONS

1. Sift flour, baking powder, salt, cocoa, and sugar into a bowl.
2. Combine sour cream, melted butter, and egg yolks in another bowl.
3. In a third bowl, beat egg whites with cream of tartar until stiff and shiny.
4. Stir ingredients of second bowl into first bowl.
5. Fold in beaten egg whites.
6. Using a medium-size spoon, place about 2 tablespoons of batter in center of heated electric waffle iron. Close top quickly so batter will not start cooking before it has spread to edges of waffle iron. Each waffle iron is different and comes with its own set of instructions for length of cooking time.

These can be served with Liz's butter: 1 stick softened butter or margarine creamed with ½ teaspoon cinnamon and 1 tablespoon honey.

Liz, age nine

When I was in second grade we had cooking class once a week. We learned how to make popcorn balls and lollipops, and we made bread for parents' night. Now I like to cook on my own, especially on Sunday mornings. My chocolate waffles are a big hit for breakfast.

When I melt the butter I hold the pan away from the heat so it won't burn. It makes such strange and wonderful sizzling noises.

Christopher usually watches from on high, but sometimes he jumps on the counter to let me know he's hungry.

If Mommy's around I ask her to help me when the time comes to fold in the egg whites. I try to keep as much air in them as possible because that's what makes the batter fluffy.

Spoon the batter onto the center of the hot waffle iron and close the top quickly so it'll spread out to the edges. There's an old expression that the first waffle never works, so don't feel discouraged if that happens to you. Practice makes perfect!

Michele's Capellini al Pomadoro e Basilico
(angel hair spaghetti with tomato and basil)
SERVES 4 AS A MAIN COURSE, 6 AS AN APPETIZER

INGREDIENTS
4–5 slices prosciutto (This is a salty Italian
    ham you can buy at a deli counter.)
½ onion
3 tablespoons olive oil
28-ounce can peeled Italian tomatoes
Salt and freshly ground pepper to taste
1-pound package capellini (or spaghettini)
2 tablespoons (¼ stick) butter
1 bunch fresh basil

UTENSILS
sharp knife
cutting board
towel for cleaning knife blade
skillet
large pot
long-handled fork for separating pasta
long-handled large spoon for
    adding sauce to pasta
colander
potholders
serving platter or bowl

INSTRUCTIONS
1. Slice prosciutto into small pieces.
2. Chop onion into small pieces.
3. Heat oil in skillet and cook prosciutto and onion for 2 minutes. By then the oil will be nice and
    hot, and the fat will have cooked off the prosciutto.
4. Add tomatoes, salt, and pepper and cook over medium heat for 20 minutes.
5. While sauce is cooking, start water boiling in pot.
6. Add half package of capellini to boiling salted water and cook for about 5 minutes.
7. Add butter and half of the basil to sauce. Stir.
8. Drain pasta in colander. Pasta must be very well drained or your sauce will get watery. Place on
    platter and mix in sauce. Decorate with remaining basil.

Michele, age eight

My father has been a restaurant chef all his life. He started studying how to be one when he was only fourteen, and he's traveled all over the world. He likes to tell people that he's cooked in every country that has a kitchen.

I hope to follow in his footsteps and have a restaurant of my own someday. Next year I'll start helping him do things like take reservations and maybe host a little bit, which means I'll show some of the people to their tables.

I usually go to his restaurant after school and we spend a few hours cooking together. He's very famous for his spaghetti sauce, and I can see why.

When you're chopping, you should try to use the tip of your knife. Daddy says I should always clean the blade, turned away from me, with a towel after I've finished cutting one thing and before I cut something else. That's so the flavors won't get all mixed up.

After you have the prosciutto and onion cooking, keep mixing them so they won't stick to the pan.

When you stir in the tomatoes, be very careful not to let them splatter into the flame or burner because if they do you can get burned.

If you push all the pasta into the water it will cook evenly. After it's been in the water a few minutes you can separate it with a long-handled fork.

Daddy says that the real secret of being a great cook is that you do it with your heart and with passion. That way you will always get great happiness from cooking.

Jessica's Teddy Bear Bread

2 BEARS

INGREDIENTS

½ cup milk

3 tablespoons sugar

2 teaspoons salt

3 tablespoons margarine

1 envelope active dry yeast

1½ cups warm water

6½–7 cups white bread flour or
all-purpose flour

Oil

8 raisins

1 egg, lightly beaten with 1 tablespoon
cold water

2 ribbons—each ribbon should be 3 feet
long and 1½ inches wide

UTENSILS

measuring cups

medium-size pot

measuring spoons

2 large mixing bowls

wooden spoon

pastry board

towel

baking sheets

toothpick or pair of scissors

pastry brush

potholders

2 cooling racks

INSTRUCTIONS

1. Pour milk into pot. Heat over medium heat until bubbles form around edge of pan. Remove from heat. Stir in sugar, salt, and margarine. Cool to lukewarm.

2. Dissolve yeast thoroughly in warm water. Pour into large mixing bowl.

3. Add milk mixture and 3 cups of the flour. Beat with wooden spoon until smooth. Stir in 3½–4 cups more flour, or enough to make a stiff dough.

4. Knead dough on floured board for 8–10 minutes. Place in bowl greased with oil; grease top lightly. Cover with towel. Let rise for 1 hour. Punch down.

5. Divide dough into four equal pieces. Set two aside for bear bodies. Cut one of the remaining pieces in half for two heads and the other one into fourteen pieces. Shape all pieces of dough into balls. Place large balls on greased baking sheets for bodies. Place medium balls above for heads. Flatten slightly. Attach small balls for paws, noses, and ears.

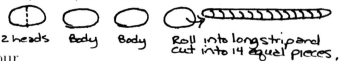

6. Cover with towel; let rise for about 1 hour.

7. Adjust rack one-third up from bottom of oven and preheat oven to 400°F. Make indentations for ears, eyes, noses, and belly buttons with end of toothpick or point of scissors. Place raisins for eyes, noses, and belly buttons.

8. Brush egg glaze on bears. Bake for 25–30 minutes. Remove from oven and cool on racks. The bears look very cute with nice bows around their necks.

Jessica, age ten

I was born in France, where homemade bread is very much a part of everyone's life. My mother baked our bread for as long as I can remember, and it looked like so much fun that I wanted to do it too.

Last year we had a baby-sitter named Jean Williams who taught me how to make teddy bear bread. I always make two of them so I can give one away to a friend.

When you're heating the milk, be sure it doesn't boil. The heat should be under the center of the pot.

Yeast is very important because it's what makes dough rise. It comes in a small package, and you should tap it a few times with your finger to keep the grains from sticking inside.

The yeast must be completely dissolved in the water before pouring it into the mixing bowl.

Mixing the dough can be messy so Mommy rolls up my sleeves.

Now comes the exhausting part…kneading the dough. You pound it for eight to ten minutes, or until it doesn't stick to your hands. Sometimes I even jump up in the air. Mommy usually helps me with this toward the end because her hands are bigger and stronger than mine. The best way to unstick your fingers is to sprinkle them with flour.

Then I oil the bowl and put the doughball into it. You have to rub a tiny bit of oil on top of the dough as well, but don't use too much because it will make it too greasy.

Put a towel on top of the bowl to keep it moist, and be sure it's not in a draft. When my mother used to make bread in France, she would make her dough rise faster by covering it with lots of coats and blankets. My grandmother used to put hers in her bed!

While our dough is taking a nap, Mommy and I clean up the kitchen and chat. She's expecting a baby in a few months so that's mostly what we talk about these days. We know it's going to be a girl, and I'm looking forward to teaching her how to bake in a few years.

After the dough has risen, you separate it into four equal parts.

Two of the pieces are for the bodies. You'll have two left; one of these gets divided in half for the heads. Roll the fourth piece into a snake and cut it with a knife into fourteen balls for ears, noses, and paws. I always look at my teddy bear drawing while I'm assembling.

Now it's time for another little snooze.

I use a toothpick to make the marks in the ears and to pierce the dough in the places where the raisins will go. Bears are cuter if the eyes are close to the nose and not too far apart. Place the eye and belly button raisins straight up and down and the nose raisins sideways.

If you paint your bears with a little egg and water they'll get a nice suntan while they're cooking. Put the bears in the lower part of the oven so they won't get too brown.

After Mommy and I tie some pretty ribbons around their necks, they're almost too lovable to eat.

David's Cheese Fried Eggs and Brownies

Cheese Fried Eggs
SERVES 1

INGREDIENTS

1–2 tablespoons butter
1 teaspoon Mrs. Dash's salt-free herb
 and spice blend
2 eggs
3 slices American cheese

UTENSILS

medium-size skillet
cup
glass plate
potholder
spatula

INSTRUCTIONS

1. Melt butter in skillet and add Mrs. Dash's salt-free herb and spice blend. Cook over medium heat. Add a little more butter.
2. Break eggs into a cup and transfer to skillet. Cook under a glass plate until whites get white. Remove plate and cover eggs with cheese. Replace plate and cook until cheese is almost melted. Turn off heat; when cheese is melted, transfer eggs to serving dish.

Brownies
16 SQUARES

INGREDIENTS

1 stick (8 tablespoons) sweet butter
2 ounces (2 squares) unsweetened chocolate
1 cup sugar
½ teaspoon vanilla extract
2 large or extra large eggs
½ cup sifted all-purpose flour
Pinch of salt

2 ounces (generous ½ cup) walnuts or pecans,
 broken into medium-size pieces (optional)
Extra walnuts or pecans, whole or broken,
 for decoration
Extra butter for greasing pan (or spray pan
 with vegetable cooking spray)

UTENSILS

8-inch square cake pan
aluminum foil
potholder or towel
pastry brush or waxed paper
saucepan or double boiler
rubber or wooden spatula

measuring cup
measuring spoons
sifter
2 cooling racks
sharp knife

INSTRUCTIONS

1. Adjust rack one-third up from bottom of oven and preheat oven to 350°F.
2. Prepare baking pan. Tear off a 12-inch square of aluminum foil, center it over the inverted pan, fold down the sides and corners, and then remove the foil and turn the pan right side up. Place the foil in the pan. In order not to tear the foil, use a potholder or a folded towel, and pressing with the potholder or towel, smooth the foil into place. Butter lightly the bottom and halfway up the sides, spreading soft or melted butter with a pastry brush or crumpled waxed paper. Set aside.
3. Place butter and chocolate in a heavy 2–3-quart saucepan over lowest heat (or in a large double boiler over hot water on moderate heat). Stir occasionally with a rubber or wooden spatula until butter and chocolate are melted and smooth. Set aside to cool for about 3 minutes and then stir in sugar and vanilla. Add eggs, one at a time, stirring until smooth after each addition. Add the flour and salt and stir until smooth. (If you like nuts in your brownies, you can stir in the walnuts or pecans.) Turn batter into prepared pan and smooth top. (If you choose to decorate the tops of the brownies with nuts, press them in now.)
4. Bake for 20–25 minutes, or until a toothpick inserted gently into the center of the cake barely comes out clean but not dry. Do not overbake. Brownies should be soft and slightly moist.
5. Set aside to cool until pan reaches room temperature. Then cover with a rack, invert, and remove pan and aluminum foil. Bottom of cake should look slightly moist in center. Cover with another rack and invert again, leaving cake right side up. It will be about ¾ inch thick.
6. Transfer cake to a cutting board and with a long, thin, sharp knife cut into squares. If cake doesn't cut neatly, transfer to freezer or refrigerator until firm and then cut it.

David, age sixteen

For me, the only drawback about loving to cook is the calories, because the whole creative process leads toward my loving what I've created, and most of the really delicious foods, I've discovered, are fattening.

Cooking is sort of like working with clay because you're molding different shapes, except I use food so I mold it into different flavors. The other part of cooking I enjoy is seeing other people get pleasure out of what I've created, and I love the compliments.

My sisters gave me a toque with my nickname, Pogy, on it and I use it when I cook because it's fun to wear and it keeps my hair out of my face. I bought myself a marble rolling pin and I'd have to say it's my most prized possession.

I have so much homework during the week that I usually cook on Saturdays, and I begin the day by cooking an invention of mine called cheese fried eggs. Then, after I've eaten breakfast, I make brownies for the rest of my family.

If the window is open when I start on the eggs I use a spatula as a windshield so the air won't blow out the flames on the burner. After the butter's melted, I sprinkle in Mrs. Dash's salt-free herb and spice blend, which I think is the most wonderful invention because you can use it in so many things like eggs, salads, spaghetti, soups—whatever. Cook over medium heat until it starts making the room smell nice and then add a little more butter so the eggs won't stick.

I always break my eggs into a cup first because I hate broken yolks and this way, if one of the yolks breaks, you can start over.

By using a glass plate to cover your eggs you can see everything that's going on. When the whites get white and start creeping over the yolks, remove the plate with a pot-holder and cover the eggs completely with three slices of American cheese. Replace the glass plate and cook until the cheese melts around the edges and toward the middle. Turn off the heat and let the eggs sit until the rest of the cheese melts, and then transfer them to a fresh plate.

The best recipe for brownies is All-American Brownies from *Maida Heatter's Book of Great Chocolate Desserts*—they're all fudgy and simply delicious and they don't taste like cake. Before I do anything else I prepare the pan. I always apply melted butter with a pastry brush because this method guarantees even buttering and, more important, it means you won't tear the aluminum foil.

It's pretty hard to burn anything in a double boiler, so I use one instead of a regular pot.

I like to make a design on the top with pecans, which I prefer to leave whole.

Sometimes it's hard to know if my twin sisters love me for my personality or for my Saturday specials.

Sarah's Hamburger Pie

ONE 9-INCH TWO-CRUST PIE

INGREDIENTS

1 package two 9-inch piecrust shells (frozen)
1 medium onion
½ red bell pepper
1 pound lean ground beef
1 can (10¾ ounces) condensed tomato soup

UTENSILS

cutting board
small, sharp knife
2 small bowls (to hold diced onion
    and pepper)
large skillet
wooden spatula
can opener for soup
fork
cookie sheet
potholders

INSTRUCTIONS

1. Preheat oven to 400°F.
2. Remove piecrust shells from freezer. Invert one shell onto waxed paper from pie shell package and remove pan. Leave other shell upright in pan.
3. Dice onion and pepper.
4. In a large skillet, brown beef in its own fat with vegetables. Drain excess fat.
5. Remove skillet from heat and stir in undiluted soup. Pour into pie shell still in pan.
6. Carefully flatten the other crust onto its waxed paper, pinching together any cracks. Invert crust over pie. Peel off waxed paper. Seal the crusts and flute the edges. Prick top crust several times with a fork.
7. Place the pie pan on a cookie sheet. Bake for 40–45 minutes, or until crust is brown. Cool for 5 minutes before cutting.

This makes a good dinner with a green salad and fruit for dessert.

Sarah, age eight

My mom started me cooking about a year ago. She taught me how to cook eggs in lots of different ways, and I also learned how to make things like fruit salad and brownies. My dad likes to cook too, and he makes all our bread on weekends when he's home from work. Making bread has always been a family activity for us—we find it relaxing and besides, it makes the whole house smell good. I help knead the dough and my little sister Annie, who's four, likes to put in the raisins.

One recipe, which I can make all by myself, is Hamburger Pie. It's easy to fix and it tastes wonderful. I usually make it for supper, and I make enough for the whole family.

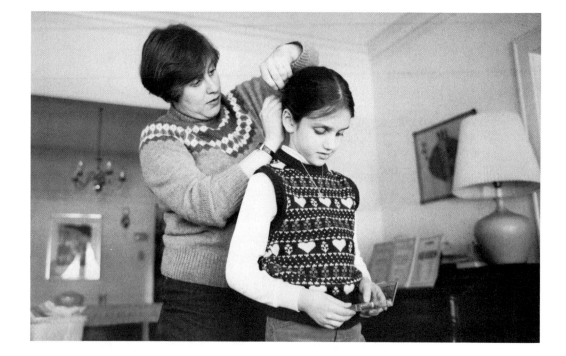

I have long hair because I'm studying ballet, and Mommy always pins it up for me so it won't get in my way.

I keep my recipes in a pretty yellow recipe box that I got for Chanukah this year. It's decorated with lots of little daisies and butterflies. Mommy got her recipe box when she was my age and she still has it. We keep them side by side in the kitchen.

There are two pie shells in a package, and I leave one of them in the aluminum pan. The other one, which is going to be used later for the top of the pie, gets turned upside down on a piece of waxed paper that's in the package.

Chopping the onion is the hardest part. You should have a wet paper towel nearby so if you start crying you can just wipe your eyes and keep on going. Remember, don't rub your eyes with your hands because they've been on the onion and it'll only make it worse. The faster you cut an onion the less you cry, but sometimes you just have to suffer a little for your art. This is definitely the heartrending part of the operation. The first time I cut an onion I cried so hard I couldn't see.

Cutting the pepper is much easier. First cut it right down the middle and rinse the seeds out of the half that you're using. Then chop it into small pieces, same as the onion.

When the second piecrust has thawed, I flatten it. It's important to have the edges all in one piece so I just pinch them together like Play-Doh.

Now we have to brown the beef. I like to put the hamburger in *before* I turn on the burner so it won't splatter and burn me. I add the onion and pepper and stir until I can't see any red in the meat. I use a wooden spatula because the handle doesn't get hot and it doesn't scratch the pan.

Opening the can of soup is the hardest for me because I'm left-handed. I'm hoping to get an electric can opener for my birthday.

Putting the pie together is my favorite part, and for this I need a stool.

The top piecrust is now a little bit larger than the pie pan so I tuck the edges of the top crust under the bottom crust, all around. And then I do the crimping, or pinching, which not only looks pretty but serves a purpose because it keeps the juices from leaking out. Last thing I do is to punch holes in the top of the crust with a fork so my pie won't explode while it's cooking.

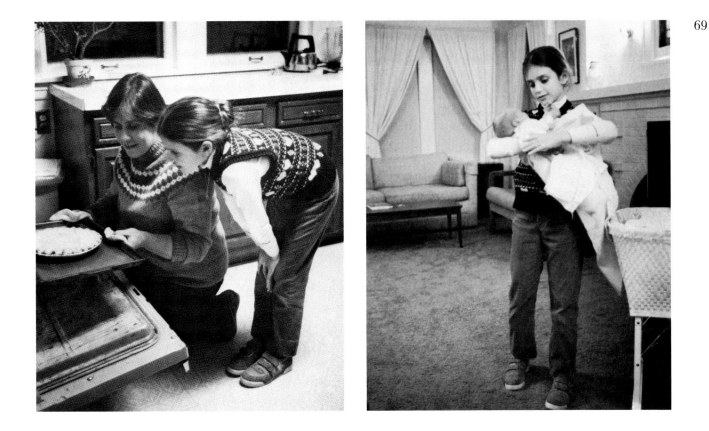

Mommy helps me put the pie in the oven. For some reason it browns best if I use a cookie sheet. Don't forget to use potholders because the oven's pretty hot by now.

While my pie's baking I like to play with our new baby, Emily. Finally, supper's ready and it's time to eat. Annie always says, "Oh no, not hamburger pie again!" because all she ever likes is pancakes or pizza.

Matthew's Disappearing Concoction
16 SQUARES

INGREDIENTS

1 stick (8 tablespoons) butter

1½ cups graham cracker crumbs

½ cup shredded or flaked coconut

1 cup (6 ounces) semisweet chocolate chips

1 can sweetened condensed milk

UTENSILS

medium-size pot

8-inch square cake pan

spoon

measuring cup

can opener

potholders

INSTRUCTIONS

1. Preheat oven to 350°F for 10 minutes.

2. Melt butter in pot and pour into cake pan.

3. With a spoon spread graham cracker crumbs evenly into pan on top of butter.

4. Pour coconut over layer of cracker crumbs.

5. Add layer of chocolate chips.

6. Pour condensed milk over top.

7. Bake for 35 minutes. Cool for at least 10 minutes before cutting into squares.

Matthew, age nine

I don't know exactly when I started cooking but it was probably when I was around six. I'd help my sister make brownies. I'm not what you'd call a gourmet cook, but I do enjoy fixing tasty snacks. My most popular after-school special is called "Disappearing Concoction," and I'm proud to say I invented it all by myself.

After you've preheated the oven, melt a stick of butter and pour it into a cake pan. You can buy graham cracker crumbs in a package, which saves time, and believe me when you're as busy as I am this is important.

Add three more layers—shredded coconut, chocolate chips, and sweetened condensed milk—and it's ready to go into the oven. The best part about making this recipe is nibbling on the ingredients as you go.

Kelly and I can hardly wait!

Rena's Cucumber Sushi

32 PIECES

INGREDIENTS

1 cup Japanese short-grain rice (This comes in
  a bag, and the most popular brand has a big
  pink flower on the package.)
1 cup plus 2 tablespoons cold water
3½–4 tablespoons sushi su (Japanese
  seasoned vinegar)
4 sheets Yakisushi-Nori (This is paper-thin
  seaweed for sushi. You can buy packages
  with 10 or 50 sheets and freeze what you
  don't use.)
1 small unwaxed cucumber (unwaxed because
  you are going to keep skins on)
Soy sauce for dipping (optional)

UTENSILS

measuring cup	fan (optional)
large bowl for rice	cloth
strainer	cutting board
small bowl for water	scissors (to cut seaweed)
electric rice cooker	sharp cutting knife

INSTRUCTIONS

1. Place rice in a bowl. Pour in cold water to cover and stir until water is very cloudy with starch. Drain rice through a strainer and repeat washing until water is clear. (The reason you are washing off the starch is because if you don't, later on when you add the vinegar it will slide off.)
2. Drain rice and put it in an electric rice cooker. Add the 1 cup plus 2 tablespoons of cold water. It will take about 20 minutes for the rice to cook, and you should wait another 15 minutes before seasoning it.
3. Turn rice out into a large bowl and fan it to get rid of all the steam. When steam is gone, toss rice with seasoned vinegar. Cover rice with damp cloth and set aside but don't put it in refrigerator—it will get hard and crusty that way.
4. Cut four pieces of seaweed in half lengthwise. Stack the eight half sheets and keep them dry.
5. Cut off ends of cucumber and slice lengthwise into eight strips.
6. Place sheet of seaweed in front of you, rough side facing up. Dampen hands and lay rice over half of seaweed that's closest to you. Place cucumber strip across middle of rice. Roll sushi up and set aside with seam facing down. Repeat to make seven more rolls. Cut each roll into four pieces.

Rena, age nine

I was born in Japan and lived there until I was five, which may explain why I care as much about how food looks as how it tastes. Even when I make something as simple as a tuna fish salad I love to make it look beautiful. It's easy to do. Use parsley sprigs for the trees, an egg and some carrots for the sun, and tuna fish for a rolling mountain.

My favorite Japanese food is cucumber sushi. Lots of people think sushi means raw fish but that's not so. Sushi is the Japanese way of saying "rice seasoned with vinegar."

You can buy all the necessary supplies—the seaweed, vinegar, rice, and probably even a fan—at any Asian grocery store.

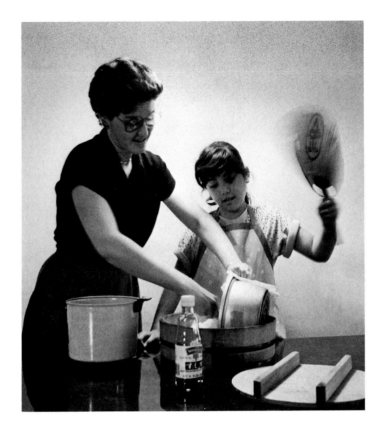

If you're the type of person who likes making something as complicated as sushi, it's probably worth it to have an electric rice cooker. Japanese rice is very difficult to cook otherwise, and with sushi you really shouldn't use any other kind. In the old days in Japan, when a woman could make a perfect bowl of rice she was ready to get married. And way back then she had to cook it on a wood-burning stove.

When the rice is cooked, transfer it to a large bowl and fan it to get rid of the steam. We use a Japanese wooden tub, but of course that's not necessary. And if you don't have a real fan, a piece of stiff cardboard is just as good. Get a friend to help toss the rice while you do the fanning. After the steam is all gone, add the seasoned vinegar and toss the rice gently with your hands. Don't be too rough or the rice will get all mushy. Then cover it with a damp cloth, and while it's resting, slice the cucumbers and cut the seaweed.

Cut each piece of seaweed in half lengthwise, and place the shiny side down. The other side, which is rough, will grip the rice, so be sure it's facing you. Now you're ready to roll. If you keep dampening your hands in a bowl of water, the rice won't stick to them.

It's also helpful to keep the knife blade moist when you're doing the final cutting.

Meshi agaré. That means "eat up" in Japanese.

Muffie's Homemade Granola
4–5 CUPS

INGREDIENTS
4 cups Old Fashioned Quaker Oats
   (uncooked)
2½ cups shredded coconut
1 cup wheat germ
1 cup chopped walnuts
1 cup sunflower seeds
1 teaspoon nutmeg
1 tablespoon cinnamon
2½ cups honey

UTENSILS
measuring cup
measuring spoons
large mixing bowl
large spoon
large, heavy skillet (preferably 2
   for quantity above)
jar with tight-fitting lid

INSTRUCTIONS
1. Measure all ingredients into mixing bowl.
2. Stir mixture until honey coats other ingredients.
3. Cook mixture in large skillet or skillets over medium heat, stirring constantly, for about 5 minutes, or until oats turn golden brown.
4. Allow granola to cool, then store for breakfasts and snacks in can or jar with tight-fitting lid.

Muffie, age eleven

I've always cooked a lot with my mother so I've learned most of what I know from her. She's from South Carolina and I'd say a lot of good cooks come from there. Don't ask me why. My father's taught me how to do bacon and eggs because that's what he does for the three of us on weekends.

I don't like to bother with cookbooks—the grown-up kind—but there is one book I particularly like called *Love at First Bite,* by Jane Cooper. It has a wonderful recipe for homemade granola. I don't follow it exactly because what I like the most about cooking is improvising to suit my own taste buds.

I enjoy shopping for all the ingredients. I go to the neighborhood health food store for the coconut, honey, sunflower seeds, cinnamon, and nutmeg. Then I go to the supermarket and buy anything else I'll need.

If I have a hard time opening the wheat germ jar—which I usually do, especially if it's a new one—I put on a rubber glove and that always seems to do the trick. Another good trick is to put a rubber band around the lid.

You can buy your walnuts already chopped, but I enjoy doing the work myself. Measuring the honey is the hardest part for me because it's so sticky. If you let the jar sit in a pot of hot water for about five minutes, the honey will pour more easily. And if you coat the measuring cup with a little bit of oil, you'll get every last drop of honey out of it.

After I mix everything together in a bowl I divide it into two skillets so I'll have plenty of room when I'm stirring. It's important to stir the granola frequently because it cooks *very* fast and you wouldn't want it to burn. I like setting one of those little timers because then I don't have to worry about how much time goes by. Granola will last a long time if you store it in an apothecary jar with a tight-fitting lid and keep it at room temperature. One trouble is, it's so delicious, it disappears in a minute in our house.

Lizzie's Pumpkin Pie

ONE 9-INCH PIE

Filling for 9-inch pie

INGREDIENTS

3 cups fresh pumpkin purée (A 3–4-pound
   pumpkin will yield about 3½ cups of purée, or you
   can substitute canned pumpkin—but don't buy
   the filling with spices if you are going to follow
   the rest of this recipe.)
½ cup sugar
2 tablespoons molasses

½ teaspoon salt
½ teaspoon nutmeg
¼ teaspoon cinnamon
1 teaspoon grated fresh gingerroot, or
   ½ teaspoon powdered ginger
3 large eggs, lightly beaten
1 cup heavy cream

UTENSILS

sharp knife
baking sheet
steamer
large pot with cover
colander

wooden spoon
food processor or blender or potato masher
measuring cup
measuring spoons
large bowl

INSTRUCTIONS

1. Preheat oven to 425°F. If you are using fresh pumpkin, cut around and discard stem. Cut pumpkin into eight pieces. Scoop
   away and discard fibers. Save seeds and put on baking sheet, sprinkle them with salt, and bake in a 350°F oven for 15 minutes, or until seeds are golden brown. Place unpeeled pumpkin pieces in top of a steamer large enough to hold them. Cover
   and steam over boiling water for about 15 minutes, or until pumpkin flesh is tender.
2. Remove pumpkin pieces from steamer, let cool until easy to touch. Scrape flesh from outer peel and discard peel. Purée
   flesh in a food processor or blender or use a potato masher.
3. Combine all filling ingredients in a mixing bowl and blend well.

Pastry dough for 9-inch pie

INGREDIENTS

1½ cups flour
¼ teaspoon salt
½ cup shortening
3–4 tablespoons cold water

UTENSILS

measuring cup
measuring spoons
mixing bowl
pastry blender or 2 knives
fork

rolling pin
wooden or marble pastry board
   for rolling dough
9-inch pie plate
potholders

INSTRUCTIONS

1. Mix the flour and salt. Cut in the shortening with a pastry blender or two knives. Combine lightly only until the mixture
   resembles coarse meal or very tiny peas: its texture will not be uniform but will contain crumbs and small bits and pieces.
2. Sprinkle water over the flour mixture, a tablespoon at a time, and mix lightly with a fork, using only enough water so that
   the pastry will hold together when pressed gently into a ball. Don't handle the pastry dough any more than necessary, or it
   will be tough: treat it firmly, not timidly, but don't fuss with it. The flour and shortening should not be blended too well: it
   is the bits of shortening left in the dough that puff and expand during baking.
3. Roll the dough out 2 inches larger than the pie pan, then fit it loosely but firmly into the pan. Crimp or flute the edges.
4. Pour filling into prepared pie shell and place in oven.
5. Bake at 425°F for 15 minutes. Reduce heat to 350°F and bake for 30–40 minutes longer, or until filling is set.

Lizzie, age fourteen

I can remember making blackberry crumble with my mother, who loves to cook, when I was about four, and ever since then I've cooked a lot—mostly desserts. My father doesn't cook at all but he's quite proud of his pancakes.

Every year just before Halloween I go shopping for pumpkins. I always buy two of them so I'll have one for a pie and one for a jack-o'-lantern.

I use Fannie Farmer's recipe for the piecrust and a version of Craig Claiborne's recipe for the filling.

Start off by cutting the pumpkin down the center with a sharp knife and then keep on dividing until you've got about eight pieces.

One reason I like to use a fresh pumpkin instead of canned for the filling is that I love to eat the seeds. Rinse them carefully and roast them with a little salt on a baking sheet until golden brown. They're delicious.

If you cut the pumpkin into little pieces it'll cook faster when you steam it. My brother Nicky just watches because he's too young to use a sharp knife.

I use a food processor to purée the pumpkin pulp, but you can use a blender or I guess you could even squish it with a potato masher.

I always add some molasses even though most recipes don't list it as an ingredient.

When you finish making the pie filling set it aside and start on the crust. You can buy them ready-made but I like making my own. Take off all your rings and bracelets and be sure to measure the flour before your hands get all messed up.

I usually make some extra dough so I can cut out a few cookies.

When the dough's rolled out you can see whether it's big enough by holding the pie
dish over it.

Transferring the dough to the dish isn't easy! But if it breaks in the process just patch it up and don't tell anybody.

It's very important to remember to lower the heat of the oven after the pie has been cooking for fifteen minutes or else the crust will cook sooner than the filling.

While you wait you can carve the other pumpkin. Or do your homework!

Max's Apple Surprise

SERVES 4

Apple Surprise

INGREDIENTS
1 cantaloupe
1 quart strawberries (you can substitute raspberries, if
    you prefer)
4 apples
1 cup lemon juice
8 mint leaves

UTENSILS
sharp knife
large spoon
1 large bowl (for cut-up fruit)
small melon-ball cutter
2 small bowls (for apple tops and apple balls)

INSTRUCTIONS
1. Cut cantaloupe in half, remove seeds, scoop out pieces of melon with melon-ball cutter, and place in large bowl. Wash strawberries, remove stems, and cut in half. Place in bowl with cantaloupe balls.
2. Wash apples, slice off stem ends, and reserve these caps in a small bowl with ½ cup of the lemon juice. With melon-ball cutter scoop out meat of apples, discarding cores, and put apple balls into other small bowl with the remaining ½ cup of lemon juice. Squeeze a little lemon into apple shells to keep them from darkening.
3. Fill apple shells with cut-up fruit, including apple balls, and spoon in some of the strawberry purée sauce (see accompanying recipe). Decorate each apple cap with two mint leaves and place on top of apples. Set apples in dessert bowls and pour a little more sauce around top of caps.

Strawberry Purée Sauce

INGREDIENTS
1 quart strawberries (you can substitute raspberries, if you
    prefer)
Artificial sweetener to taste (each packet equals 2 teaspoons
    of sugar) (optional)
¼ cup water
Juice of ½ lemon

UTENSILS
blender
fine-mesh strainer
bowl
small ladle

INSTRUCTIONS
1. Wash strawberries and cut off stems.
2. Dissolve artificial sweetener in water.
3. Purée berries and dissolved sweetener in blender.
4. Strain sauce into bowl, bearing down on it in strainer with ladle to push through all the fruit. Stir in lemon juice.

Max, age nine

My parents both cook and ever since I can remember I've always loved to be in the kitchen. The first time I ever cooked anything was when I was about six—I made a quiche.

What I like best about cooking is making up stuff that tastes good. I think that in order to be a creative cook you have to be an adventurous eater and be willing to try almost anything. I love going to foreign restaurants and trying exotic things like chicken's claws or jellyfish.

Our entire family is on a health kick, which is why we all love Michel Guérard's Apple Surprise.

It's fun if you use different color apples—green, yellow, and red. You need to have two bowls with lemon juice in them—one for the apple tops and one for the pieces of apple that you scoop out of the apples. This keeps them from turning brown. I usually make fresh juice from real lemons, but if you want you can use the kind that comes in a bottle.

The apples get filled with fruit—I prefer to use only cantaloupe and strawberries. Put the lids back on and add two little mint leaves for decoration.

Now it's time to make the sauce. After you've washed the strawberries and cut off the stems, you feed the berries slowly into a blender and add a little lemon juice. Don't forget to put the top on, or you'll be decorating your whole kitchen instead of just the apples.

The blender always lets you know if it's having a hard time. If it doesn't sound happy, add a little water or fruit juice.

When you strain the purée, don't push too hard with the ladle because the whole point is to keep the seeds from going through. Mommy keeps saying, "You don't have to kill it, Max."

After I pour a little strawberry purée into each apple, I put on the tops and add a little more. Then I make Popsicles with whatever's left over.

I think my father has ESP because the minute the apples are ready he always appears, like magic, saying, "Don't you need a taster?"

Stephanie's Lemon Chicken and Strawberry Parfait

SERVES 4

Lemon Chicken

INGREDIENTS
3½-pound chicken
1 lemon
1 teaspoon oregano
1 teaspoon dill weed
1 teaspoon dried rosemary
1 teaspoon dried basil
1 teaspoon paprika

UTENSILS
sharp knife for trimming fat
roasting pan
aluminum foil
spoon for basting
timer
potholders

INSTRUCTIONS
1. Preheat oven to 400°F. Wash chicken and remove excess fat. Line roasting pan with aluminum foil and place chicken in it.
2. Cut lemon in half and rub chicken inside and out with one half. Place same lemon half in front of chicken's cavity as a cup to catch spices.
3. Sprinkle chicken and lemon cup with oregano, dill, rosemary, basil, and paprika. Place lemon cup inside chicken.
4. Squeeze juice of the remaining lemon half over entire chicken so you have some juice in pan for basting. Add 2 tablespoons of water to pan. Some chickens are fatter than others, so add more water if the pan gets dry.
5. Bake chicken at 400°F for 15 minutes. Baste chicken and reduce heat to 350°F. Continue basting every 15 minutes. Cook for about 1 hour, or until chicken is nicely browned. If clear juices run out when you pierce chicken leg, chicken is cooked.

Strawberry Parfait

INGREDIENTS
1 package strawberry Jell-O
4 strawberries
8 ounces Cool Whip (or fresh whipped cream)

UTENSILS
mixing bowl for Jell-O
4 parfait or wine glasses
small, sharp knife for removing stems from strawberries
    and cutting them in half
mixing bowl for Cool Whip
spoon
measuring cup

INSTRUCTIONS
1. Make Jell-O according to directions on package.
2. Fill parfait glasses halfway and place in refrigerator on a slant.
3. Remove stems from strawberries and cut berries in half lengthwise. Set aside.
4. Combine remaining Jell-O with Cool Whip, reserving small portion of Cool Whip for final decoration.
5. When Jell-O is firm, remove from refrigerator, add pink Jell-O–Cool Whip combination, and top with dollop of Cool Whip and two strawberry halves, one on each side of dollop.

Stephanie, age fifteen

I'm an only child so I've always entertained myself by cooking. When I was little, I used to surprise my mother by doing little things in the kitchen. Besides that, my god-mother, Norma Deardon, wrote a book about Southern cooking called *Spoonbread and Strawberry Wine,* and she's taught me a lot about food.

Both my parents work so it's helpful if I can make dinner when I get home from school. My best main course is baked lemon chicken, and for dessert it's fun to make straw-berry parfaits. I saw them once on television, and they looked so pretty I figured out on my own how to duplicate them.

I start with dessert, to give it time to jell. Just follow the directions on the box to make the Jell-O; if you're in a hurry, you can use ice cubes instead of cold water to make it jell faster. Pour half of the Jell-O into four pretty glasses and put them in the icebox on a slant. Mix the remaining Jell-O with most of the contents of an eight-ounce container of Cool Whip, but save a little of the Cool Whip so you can have some pure white dollops for the final topping. Slice a few strawberries in half and decorate the tops of the parfaits.

Even chickens have fat on them—it's yellow and yucky looking and you have to cut it off. And don't forget to remove the little bag with the liver and stuff in it.

After you've rubbed the chicken all over, inside and out, with half a lemon, place the same lemon half just in front of the cavity and sprinkle everything with various herbs and spices. The little lemon cup now gets put inside of the chicken, and when it gets hot it releases all the nice flavors and smells.

Basting is what keeps a chicken moist, and I set a timer so I'll remember to do it every fifteen minutes. Serve it hot from the oven!

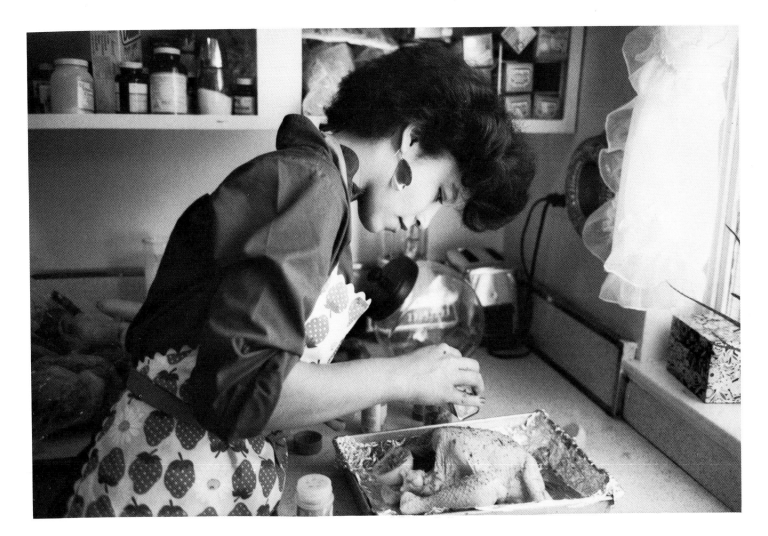

Jake's Tortillas
4 MEDIUM-SIZE TORTILLAS

INGREDIENTS

4 ounces Monterey Jack cheese

4 ounces mild Cheddar cheese

4 tortillas (Tortillas come in three different
    sizes: small, medium, and large. I buy the
    medium. They are made out of corn or
    flour. The corn ones really taste like corn
    and they're drier. I prefer flour tortillas
    because they're softer and easier to roll.)

1 small can (4¼-ounces) chopped black olives

UTENSILS

cheese grater

3 plates (1 for each cheese and 1 for finished
    tortillas)

knife

potholders

INSTRUCTIONS

1. Preheat oven or toaster oven to 350°F.
2. Shred each cheese onto a plate.
3. Place tortilla on a third plate or on toaster oven tray. Add layer of chopped olives, then layer of
    each cheese. Do the same for the rest of the tortillas.
4. Bake for about 10 minutes, or until cheeses are melted and bubbly. (Length of cooking time
    depends on how hard cheese is.) Roll or slice into pieces like a pizza.

Jake, age twelve

On weekends I spend most of my free time bike riding, and whenever I get hungry I just ride home for a quick pit stop. I try not to eat sweets or junk food, so a cheese and olive tortilla is perfect. They don't take long to make and they taste great. Another big plus is there's not a big mess to clean up.

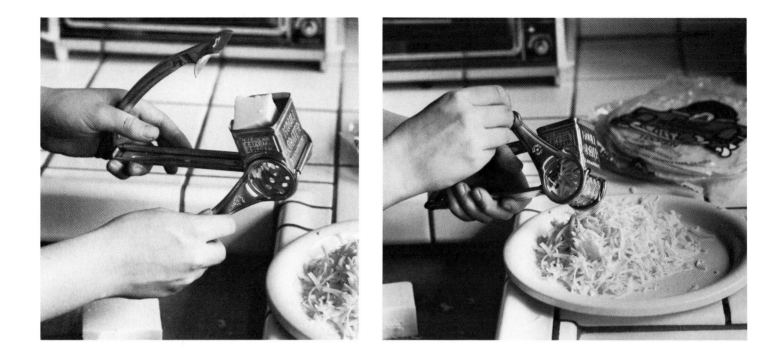

Start off by shredding the cheeses. A Mouli grater is fun to use and safe for your fingers.

I put the chopped olives on first so the cheese will melt over them. Add a layer of one cheese, then the other, and of course you're free to add anything else that suits your taste—sautéed chopped beef, diced chili peppers, or tomato sauce, to name a few possibilities. It's a great way to clean out your refrigerator.

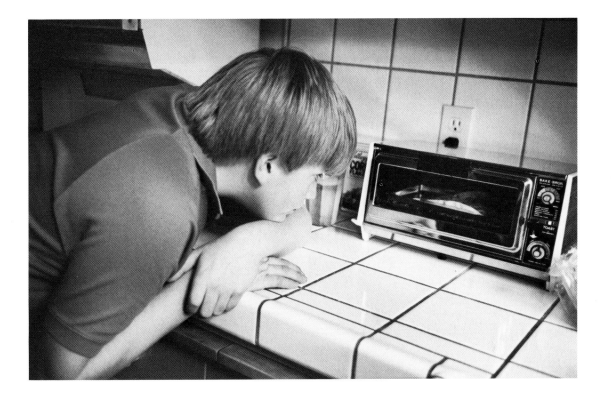

If you have a toaster oven you can watch what's going on. It's also faster because the heat's more concentrated. If you're in a real hurry, and you can keep an eye on your tortilla, you can broil it instead of bake it. When all the layers of cheese are melted, the tortilla is ready.

Sometimes I roll it up, but other times I leave it flat and cut it into eight little sections like a pizza.

Rocky's Whole Egg Pasta

SERVES 4

INGREDIENTS
1 extra large egg
4 tablespoons olive oil
2½ teaspoons salt
¾–1 cup all-purpose flour

UTENSILS
measuring spoons
large bowl
fork
measuring cup
wooden spoon
plastic wrap
hand-cranked pasta machine
some sort of pasta drying rack (can be just a long rod put
    across 2 tall jars)
huge pot
long-handled fork for testing
colander
potholders

INSTRUCTIONS
1. Mix egg, 1 tablespoon of the olive oil, and ½ teaspoon of the salt in bowl. Add flour slowly, mixing with hands, until dough forms a ball and is soft and pliable and doesn't stick to your hands anymore.
2. Wrap in plastic wrap and let rest for 30 minutes.
3. Remove from plastic wrap and pat dough. If it's sticky, roll lightly in a little more flour.
4. Separate into two balls and flatten. Put first through kneading part of pasta machine, opening it to its widest aperture. Put through twice, feeding it steadily. Then change aperture to next smaller. Continue this process until pasta has passed through narrowest aperture and is long and translucent. (If the dough turns crumbly and starts making holes, throw out and start again. The texture at the very beginning is the most important—silky soft, but not sticky—and it depends on the egg. Once you've added too much flour, the only way to change the balance is to add another whole egg and double the recipe.) If dough is too sticky, add a bit of flour. If dough crumples up or bulges as you put it through, don't worry. It is tough and elastic. Just play with it, passing it through again until it smooths out.
5. When pasta is long and delicate and translucent, cut into strips that are about 18 inches long and put each strip through cutting side of machine. This may take two people—one to feed it through and turn the handle, the other to lead it out on the other side. The pasta goes through this process only once; when it's through, hang it up on drying rack. You can cook it at once or let it dry for several hours. I like it cooked at once—it's like butter.
6. In a huge pot bring water to a boil with the remaining 3 tablespoons of olive oil and the remaining 2 teaspoons of salt. Add pasta to pot. When water returns to a boil, cook pasta for 3–4 minutes. Drain in colander and serve immediately.

Can be served with salt, pepper, butter, and grated Parmesan cheese.

Rocky, age twelve

The first thing I ever cooked by myself was biscuits. They're called baking powder biscuits, and I left out the baking powder. Everyone in my family sat around pretending they were delicious. Actually, they weren't all that bad—they were just a bit heavy because they didn't rise.

I think it's really fun to be able to eat something you've made all by yourself, something that's entirely yours. Cooking can be a very creative endeavor. It isn't quite as free as painting because there are certain rules you have to follow—you have to put flour in a cake, and you have to put yeast or baking powder in bread—but you can still do a lot to make whatever you're making your own creation.

I love doing everything from scratch, and the more complicated it is, the more fun I have. That's one of the reasons I make my own pasta. The other is that it's really better than even the best store-bought varieties.

When the ball of dough feels like a soft, heavy snowball that doesn't stick to your hands, wrap it tightly in a piece of plastic wrap and let it sit in a bowl for about thirty minutes. This lets the moisture soak through and will make the dough get tougher and more elastic.

Then, after you've unwrapped the ball, you can sprinkle it with flour once again before you flatten it enough to feed it into the pasta machine. As you keep repeating this process keep adding flour whenever the dough starts to feel sticky and be very gentle so it won't stretch too much. If you haven't done this before, it helps if you have someone turn the handle on the machine while you support both ends of the pasta. It'll be almost seven feet long when you're finished, and it should be almost translucent.

When you feed the pasta back into the opposite end of the machine, it comes out as spaghetti or, if you use a wider opening, as fettuccine. I hang it on a rack while I'm working and then lower it all into a large pot of boiling water.

The real secret of good pasta is not to cook it too long. When you make your own spaghetti it cooks faster than the packaged kind because it's fresher. I find that three or four minutes is just perfect. Be very careful when you transfer it to the colander because steam can really burn. Make sure you pour it so the steam goes away from your face.

Our cat, Tiptree, has a most sophisticated palate, and he's very fond of homemade anything.

Jason's Doggie Biscuits
ABOUT 30 LARGE BONES

INGREDIENTS

3½ cups unbleached all-purpose flour

2 cups whole-wheat flour

1 cup rye flour

2 cups bulgur (cracked wheat)

1 cup cornmeal

½ cup instant nonfat dry milk

4 teaspoons salt

1 envelope active dry yeast

¼ cup warm water

3 cups chicken broth

2–3 tablespoons shortening, margarine, or
  butter, for greasing cookie sheets

1 egg, lightly beaten with 1 teaspoon of milk,
  for basting

UTENSILS

plastic scoop for getting flour out
  of package
measuring cups
measuring spoons
wooden spoon
large mixing bowl
rolling pin

large cutting board or table with surface
  appropriate for cutting
1 large Milk-Bone (about 3½ inches)
  for tracing
cookie sheets
small bowl for egg-milk mixture
pastry brush

INSTRUCTIONS

1. Preheat oven to 300°F. Mix first 7 ingredients with a wooden spoon in large bowl.
2. Dissolve yeast thoroughly in warm water (110–115°F). Add to dry ingredients.
3. Add chicken broth to flour mixture. Stir until dough forms.
4. Roll out dough until it is ¼ inch thick. Using a large dog biscuit for a model, cut out bone shapes from dough. Place on greased cookie sheet.
5. Brush dough with egg glaze.
6. Bake bones for 45 minutes. Turn oven off. Biscuits should remain in oven overnight to harden.

Jason, age eight

You can't imagine how delicious homemade doggie bones are. The only reason I don't eat them myself is because they're made with chicken broth and I'm a vegetarian.

It makes it more fun when there are a lot of ingredients because the recipe takes a long time, and the longer it takes the more I get to do.

Opening the can of broth is the hardest part for me, and my father always helps me with that. I think men should cook the same as girls.

The part I like best is cutting out the doggie biscuits. That's the part Little Clown likes best too.

I know I won't have to clean up all alone.

After you bake your biscuits for forty-five minutes, you're supposed to turn off the oven and leave them there overnight so they'll get good and hard.

A dog's best friend is definitely his private chef.

A NOTE ON THE TYPE

This book was set in a type face called Bulmer, a replica of a type long famous in the history of English printing. It was designed and cut by William Martin in about 1790 for William Bulmer of the Shakespeare Press. In design it is all but a modern face, with vertical stress, sharp differentiation between the thick and thin strokes, and nearly flat serifs. The decorative italic shows the influence of Baskerville, as Martin was a pupil of John Baskerville's.

Composed by
Characters Typographic Services Inc.,
New York, New York

Printed and bound by
Halliday Lithographers,
Hanover, Massachusetts

Typography by Tasha Hall,
aided by previous designs